INTRODUCTION

Sheltered by the Pennine Hills, Leeds in West Yorkshire is the world centre for ready made clothing; the woollen trade is the main industry among others such as clock-making, furniture and chemicals. Three miles north west of the city is Kirstall Abbey where the monks pioneered such industries as mining for iron ore, spinning, weaving and potting, contributing to the subsequent growth of the town in the Middle Ages. Wool has predominated in the area for centuries. Sheep have grazed the Yorkshire Moors and the fast flowing streams of the Pennines have provided lime-free water ideal for the many processes of supplying wool. The cottage craft industry moved to the mills after the introduction of machinery. The main wool centres gravitated towards the valleys of the Rivers Aire, Calder and Colne owing to the coal fields supplying a source of fuel for steam power. Bradford seduced the worsted trade from Norwich and became Britain's largest wool market. Its streets tumble towards the centre, an impressive sight with its Wool Exchange and town hall.

Harrogate and Knaresborough sit in the fertile vale of North Yorkshire, the surrounding landscape being more tranquil than the industrial south west. The former is a spa town and well-known conference centre; it has dignified Victorian architecture and a well-planned centre, with notable flower borders round the "Stray". The latter sits where the River Nidd curls round a sandstone cliff, where Mother Shipton's cave can be seen and where the ruins of a 14th century castle dominate the clifftop.

To the north of Harrogate there are wonderful views sweeping westwards towards the Dales.

CONTENTS

UNDERSTANDING THE MAP	4
PATHS AND OLD ROADS	5
TOWNS AND VILLAGES	11
PLACE NAMES	14
CANALS AND RIVERS	16
CASTLES, CHURCHES AND HALLS	18
RAILWAYS	21
ANCIENT SITES	27
NATURE	28
INDUSTRIAL ARCHAEOLOGY	30
TOURIST INFORMATION	34

The gala at Barnsley, South Yorkshire (Picture: D. Widdicombe)
Leeds Town Hall (Picture: YHTB)

© Alan Kind 1990. All rights reserved. No part of this publication may be reproduced without the prior permission of David & Charles plc. Typeset by Typesetters (Birmingham) Ltd, Smethwick, West Midlands and printed in Great Britain by Redwood Press Ltd, Melksham, Wiltshire for David & Charles plc   Brunel House   Newton Abbot   Devon

UNDERSTANDING THE MAP

Any spot on a Landranger 1/50,000 map can be located by use of a National Grid reference. This is done by noting which vertical line falls to the left of the location and then which horizontal line falls below the location. For example, if we had arranged to meet a friend at *Little Alms Cliff* this falls within the one kilometre square labelled 230520.

We next estimate tenths of a square to the right of the vertical grid line, and tenths of a square above the horizontal grid line, to give a standard six figure grid reference which, in this case, is 232523. You may find it helpful to imagine nine vertical lines and nine horizontal lines in each small square when doing this. On the ground these imaginary lines represent squares of one hundred metres edge (about a hundred and ten old fashioned yards).

Some important guide books, such as those of the National Trust and the Ramblers Association, now use map references and from these the exact location of anything from a stately home to a farmhouse offering bed and breakfast can be identified.

Here is another example. If we wish to refer to the *Swastika Stone* (an Iron Age sculptured rock) in kilometre square 090460 then, by estimating tenths of a square, we get the full six-figure reference 095469.

This is all that is needed by way of referencing on a single Landranger map although, by adding letters to a reference, one can specify anywhere in Britain, on any modern Ordnance Survey (OS) map, of any scale. If you are interested in doing this, look at the instructions in the margin of the map.

Here is a useful hint for reading and measuring OS map references: "across the plain and up the hill". This will remind you to run your eye horizontally from left to right to get the "Eastings" before you run your eye from bottom to top to get the "Northings". Remember that the hints tell you which way you must run your eyes NOT which way the grid lines run!

Right, what is the six figure OS reference for *The Hollies* which is in the top right hand corner of the map? Next what feature is located by 126451? If you get these two OS references right you can get any OS references right.

(Answers: *The Hollies* is at 379595. The OS reference 126451 gives the site of *The Twelve Apostles* stone circle).

Reading a map reference

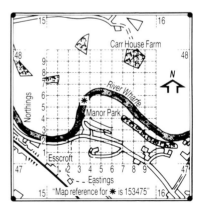

4

PATHS AND OLD ROADS

Almost half of this map being covered by the West Yorkshire conurbation, it seems appropriate to start our exploration at the pleasant outer suburb of Bingley (115395), a former market town which still keeps its livestock market, and has easy access to the countryside.

Altar Lane, Bingley – South over the Aire bridge by the wooded gorge just off the town centre is the Harden Valley with its impressive Hewenden Viaduct on the disused railway line there. A short distance up the B6429 the green road of Altar Lane takes off to the right, climbing steadily through the trees and skirting the beautiful public estate of St. Ives, accessible by stile from the lane. Fine views open up along the Aire Valley to the hills beyond Skipton. A prominent rock outcrop known as the Druids' Altar gives the lane its name, though it is questionable if Druids ever practised there; certainly they would have needed to be of an athletic turn to do so. The lane, used in the 1920s by an international motorcycle trial, once linked Bingley to the then main road from Bradford to Keighley via Harden village, and many enjoyable footpaths abound in the valley, some remarkably remote and rocky for a place so near to Bradford city centre.

Haworth Old Road and the Road of the Stoups – Away to the southwest, Haworth village needs no publicity here, but less well known is the old road to Hebden Bridge, skirting the reservoir (015353). This unsurfaced way was superseded by the 1814 turnpike now A.6033, known as the Road of the Stoups – stone pillars directing the way over the 1400ft summit. These can still be seen on the northern slope. The views in each direction are superb, the long plateaux of the South Pennines contrasting with the more rounded hills of the nearer Yorkshire Dales. East of A6033 is a third scenic moorland crossing, the direct route from the Worth Valley to Halifax by an old paved road on the summit of which a 100 yard stretch of rough paving remains. Unsigned, leaving A6033 at 028345 above Oxenhope, this road would have been used by "broggers" – packhorsemen acquiring wool from the farms for sale to the mills. Withins Inn on the 1400ft level (not to be confused with the Withins farmhouse of Brontë associations) supplied their needs en route, and

An old milestone (Knaresborough–Ilkley) looking towards March Ghyll reservoir (Ref: 1251. Picture: R. McConnell)

5

Owen and Bowen's Road Map of 1720–1764

still refreshes today's travellers.

Rombalds Moor Tracks – Returning to Bingley, north of the town lies the extensive massif of Rombalds Moor, named after the legendary giant who among other exploits is said to have kicked off the Calf rock above Ilkley from its mother the Cow. Ilkley Moor of the Yorkshire National Anthem forms the central portion of this moorland, which has seen human settlements from prehistoric times, as witness the many stone circles and other relics, and the several crossings of the moor will have been in use from those early times.

Best known is the track starting at Dick Hudson's Inn (124421) which after a short distance carries an interesting stretch of stone paving dating from the more recent packhorse age of pre-Industrial Revolution days, one set of stones for the drover being raised above the accompanying line. Keighley Gate, marked on the map as Whetstone Gate (*Gate* of course meaning *highway* in this context) was shown as a metalled motor road on the old Popular Edition O.S.1″ but it is doubtful if anything short of a 4WD safari type vehicle or a trail motorbike would tackle the rough crossing now.

The most attractive route, in the writer's view, is the most westerly, starting at Holden Gate (069440) and going by bridleway past Black Pots farmhouse and on by Doubler Stones to Windgate Nick to descend to Addingham. Scattered below Rivock Edge were once old coal pits, shallow drift mines from which the miners would repair to

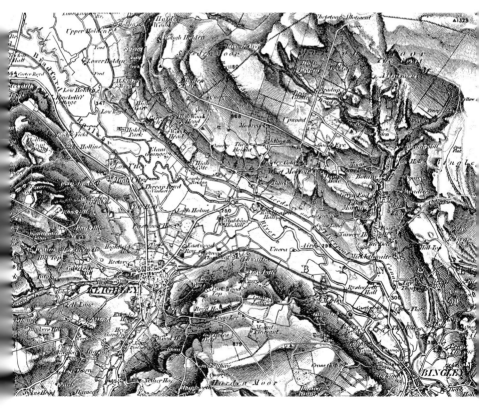

Part of David & Charles 1st Edition OS Map, Sheet No 22

Black Pots, then an ale-house, to slake their thirst.

Roman Road from Ilkley to Skipton

– Addingham itself lies on the line of the Roman Road from Ilkley (Olicana) to Ribchester via Skipton, and though lost from Ilkley, the course of the road can be picked up at Lumb Gill (083487) by a rather tenuous footpath likely to be further disjointed by the projected local bypass. The Roman Road crosses the A6034 to make up onto Addingham Low Moor and Draughton Moor and so to Skipton, with some good views on the way.

Barden Moor Bridleway

– At Skipton we must borrow Landranger No. 103 to find the start of the bridleway across Barden Moor, the one acknowledged right of way across this part of the Bolton Abbey estate, and one wonders how many more of the several permissive tracks over Barden Moor and Barden Fell (check with the estate office or the National Park Centre at Grassington for close season dates) should in fact carry public rights, the Barden Moor bridleway itself having been denied until a few years ago.

Some strange legends have grown up around this track from Rylstone to Bolton Abbey, all concerning a white doe said to roam over it. Some held the animal carried the soul of one of the Norton family of Rylstone who died in the ill-fated Catholic Rising in the North during the first Elizabeth's reign. Others declared that it was the re-incarnation of an early benefactress of Bolton Abbey, Alice de Romilly, whose son was drowned in the treacherous Strid on the River Wharfe there, but the most charming version is surely that which has Emily, one of the Norton daughters, making annual pilgrimage to pray for her brothers, accompanied by her pet white doe.

The Badgergate

– Between Bolton Abbey and Ilkley lies another attractive stretch of moorland, along the southern fringe of which runs an ancient trade route known as the Badgergate. Badger in this context signifies a pedlar or itinerant trader carrying goods between the Dales farms and the more populated lowlands beyond Harrogate. Starting from Bolton Bridge, the route goes over the shoulder of Beamsley Beacon (094517) by minor road, to take to the moor at Wards End, then across Long Ridge to Bow Shaw where the clear line is lost, these moors being subject to many alterations in the tracks of late years, by reason of disputes on rights of way allied to new landrover roads for shooting purposes.

One gains the onward way above the shooting hut at Crow Well on Denton Moor by means of a stile access to skirt the conifer plantation above March Ghyll reservoir, and up the steep hillside to

Old milestone near Harrogate, note the old spelling

another stile. An easier if longer way is cut off but runs along the footpath to the West Moorhouses (124507) and across Dearncombe Beck, then due north from Hollingley Farm, the Denton Moor shooting hut being visible on the hillside most of the way. This may well have been the alternative Low Badgergate route, but the old path below the shooting hut has now quite disappeared. The High route is followed up onto Lippersley Pike, unmarked on the map but easily identifiable by the stone shooting butt on its summit, where there is also an interesting boundary stone relating to the ancient Knaresborough Forest, hunting grounds of royalty. The stone bears the inscription K.F.1767, the date of enclosure of the forest lands.

Forest of Knaresborough Tracks – Badgergate continues over Ellercarr Pike to the Sourby crossroads, thence across the Washburn Valley with its extensive reservoir complex and many plea-

Packhorse Bridge over the River Wharfe at Ilkley (Picture: R. McConnell)

sant footpaths radiating from a delightful, pine-fringed car park. Penny Pot Lane, the straight road parallel with the A.59, carries the Badgergate, but a diversion by the green road south at 215552, near Willow House, leads to another possible alternative, and the intriguing site of John of Gaunt's hunting lodge on a bluff above a small reservoir, all part of the old Knaresborough Forest. One may wonder what a prominent Lancastrian was doing in White Rose country; he had in fact been granted the castle and associated lands of Knaresborough by his father, Edward III, and as John seems to have been one of the nicer barons of his time, perhaps he was not too unacceptable to the descendants of the Brigantes tribe who had given the Romans so much trouble in these parts.

Mention of the Romans brings us back to Blubberhouses, where by taking the track up onto the moor from the Manor House (167554) and keeping fairly close to the wall on the left, one can come across part of the Roman road that once crossed the moor from Ilkley to Aldborough, and now resembles an outsize heather-covered speed hump like the smaller versions beloved of anti-motor authorities.

North of Blubberhouses, by the new Thruscross reservoir that covers some wild raspberry-lined lanes, lies the start of a very interesting old Forest road (129593) that crosses Pockstones Moor into Wharfedale, firm easy going at first, resolving into much bog and roughery. On the other side of the reservoir, a splendid minor motor road, formerly known as Sandy Gate runs north west straight as a Roman road, up to the wild country of Greenhow Hill.

Otley Chevin and Points East

– The southern extremity of Knaresborough Forest stretched to Otley Chevin, crowned by a prehistoric track, now a minor road known as Yorkgate, giving from the public car park opposite the Royalty Inn a far-reaching view over the breezy upland country of the Forest west of Harrogate. Yet another Roman Road, from Ilkley to Tadcaster, is thought to have run some half a mile south of Yorkgate, but its line is now almost entirely lost, one short stretch near Scarcroft being taken over by a bridleway opposite the Hetchell's Wood Nature Reserve (379423).

We are now in the rolling country verging on the Vale of York, and since in enclosed agricultural terrain footpaths appearing on the map may not always be passable on the ground, the best way to explore this north-eastern sector on foot is probably to follow the Ebor Way, one of those long-distance footpaths devised to help present-day countrygoers, and something of a mixed blessing in open hill country, but having the virtue in the lowlands that one knows the recommended paths have been walked. Parts of the Ebor Way are marked on the map, but at present no comprehensive literature exists, the Dalesman book outlining the route being now out of print. It is, however, possible at Ilkley, where the Way starts off for the ultimate destination of York via Wetherby (395485), to get one's map marked by the Tourist Information Bureau staff. The public library next door has a copy of the Dalesman book by one J.K.E. Piggin of York, who devised the Way, which at the time of writing does not seem to have been taken up by the countryside authorities, though this may be remedied in the near future.

TOWNS AND VILLAGES

Bradford (1633) is in the Pennines between the River Aire and Calder centred in a shallow natural bowl and now a city with a population of nearly half a million people. Its history is best put into perspective by reference to earlier populations: in 1800 there were 13,000, in 1850 100,000 and in 1900 280,000. Bradford lies on the Roman road from Fleetwood via Ribchester and Elsack (near Skipton) to York. It was part of the Saxon manor of Gamel and there is a piece of a Saxon cross in the cathedral. The town is recorded in the Domesday Book and there was a 'chapel in the wood' on the site of the present cathedral built between 1090 and 1210, a sign of a settled community. Near the Roman road, at Barnoldswick (map 103), there was a Cistercian abbey from 1147 which moved in 1152 to Kirkstall (2536). Did the monks walk this Roman road seeking the most favourable site? Many monasteries were introduced into England from France after the 1066 Conquest and the immigrant monks brought agricultural and building crafts with them. They traditionally organised agriculture and, in the Pennines, sheep rearing would be more suitable than other types of farming; wool industries developed as simply organised, domestic industries. The church was rebuilt from 1438, another signal of commercial prosperity. In the 1530s Leland records that *'Bradforde is a praty quik market toune. It standeth much by clothing'*. During the Civil War most of the population supported the Parliamentarians and, in consequence, the town suffered little structural damage but there followed a decline in trade though it recovered during the reign of William and Mary (1689–1702). In 1760 the first bank was opened, in 1773 the Piece Hall, where domestic weavers offered for sale their pieces of cloth, was completed and in 1798 Messrs Ramsbottom, Swaine and Murgatroyd constructed the first powered mill. It is from this time that expansion accelerated, as illustrated by the population figures. There were five power mills by 1810 and 120 by 1840 and the town became an international worsted centre. Stone quarrying was successful and there were exports of stone to Sydney, Hong Kong and Calcutta. Administratively it has remarkable achievements: it was the first to have a school board, school medical services school baths, school meals and twon electricity supply.

Knaresborough Castle was besieged by Parliament's troops in the Civil War, 1644

Leeds (3033) is the county's largest town and has a rather similar history to that of neighbouring Bradford. Both have grown at the same time with wool, iron, mining and manufacturing trades. There have been determined attempts since 1850 to provide an impressive, spacious town centre and this has met with commendable success, beginning with the large, classical Town Hall of 1854 with giant Corinthian columns, which was opened by Queen Victoria and Prince Albert in 1858. The spacious Headrow followed in 1925 and they and other buildings provide an agreeable setting for a flourishing commercial centre.

Saltaire (1438) is in the River Aire valley, through which the Leeds and Liverpool canal also miraculously threads its passage. It is named after Sir Titus Salt. He moved his alpaca and mohair manufacturing mill from Bradford in 1853 to a new, huge factory here in open fields and formed a model village including 800 well appointed workers' houses and a church.

Fulneck (2232) is the site of a 1742 Moravian settlement. The Moravians were emigrant Hussite Protestants (from Moravia), and they have a self-contained community which includes a boarding school. There is a Moravian chapel at Wyke (1526).

Ilkley (1048) is a settlement of great antiquity with Anglo-Saxon remains and a 13th century church. It is in the River Wharfe valley in an agricultural area. In 1840 springs, thought to have medicinal properties, were noted and a spa was developed which includes much 19th and 20th century architecture.

Wakefield (3320) is the West Yorkshire administrative centre in the River Calder valley where it used to be an important port. A river crossing place from early times, a bridge was built in 1350 with nine pointed arches and a chantry chapel of which there are only three others. It has been much rebuilt and the original facade was re-erected in Kettlethorpe Hall as part of an elegant boathouse in 1847. Such chapels were for use by travellers, and collections assisted both chapel and bridge maintenance. Wakefield had important weaving and dyeing trades from the 13th century and was a commercial woollen cloth centre before the ascent of Leeds and Bradford. Both cloth and grain were shipped from the port. The Elizabethan Exhibition Gallery is the Old Grammar School of 1591 and now displays series of art exhibitions. The Wakefield Museum was designed as a Music Salon in 1820 and displays archeological, historical and natural history materials. In Wood Street are the 1880 Town Hall, the 1898 County Hall and the 1810 court house.

Harrogate (3055) is widely noted for the expanses of open lawns around the town centre – the 200-acre Stray, West Park and other sites where developments are forbidden. The town began following the noting in 1571 of the Tewit Spring by Sir William Slingsby on his estate issuing water tasting like medicinal waters on the continent. In 1598 Timothy Bright called this an English 'spa' after the Belgian town name, coining a new word into the English language. Originally, the waters were delivered to houses in barrels but after 1800 commercial development began. The well on the Stray has been covered since 1842 by a dome supported on Tuscan columns transferred from the Pump Room. St John's Well on the Stray is the site of another well. The Grecian style Pump Room of 1842 at the junction of Swan Road and Crescent Road contained the first public bath. This was superseded by the Royal Baths in Crescent Road built in 1897 to offer more comprehensive facilities. Since 1969 these have provided steam baths, hot, very hot and warm chambers, rest room, cold plunge and massage rooms. Hotels were built to provide appropriate accommodation and, with the reduction of the spa trade, have encouraged conferences, for which there is also a large, new and very costly conference centre.

Knaresborough (3557) has a medieval market square still with some street cobbles and an ancient cross. The castle was rebuilt from 1310 and there are Norman parts of the church. At a strategic crossing of the River Nidd, now with high-arched bridges, the town has also been a weaving centre and had the oldest linen mill.

St. John's Well on the Stray at Harrogate (Picture: S. S. Kind)

PLACE NAMES

The earliest layer of names on English maps dates from the arrival of the Celts about three thousand years ago. These names are more common in the North and West. Then, after the Roman occupation, it was the coming of the Angles and Saxons (5th to 7th centuries) which provided the chief source of place-names. Finally a layer of Scandinavian names was given to parts of North and East England by the Danish conquests (9th century) and the raids of the Norsemen (10th century).

Leeds was originally the name of a district but then the name became restricted to the chief place in it. It is very old, pre-English, and probably means "river". A likely interpretation then would be "district on the river". The river in question would be what is now called the *Aire*. Aire itself is another very old name and it probably means "strong river".

Bradford is the "broad ford". The name *Harrogate* (300550) has evolved from the nearby hill, *Harlow*, or "grey hill" and from the addition of the Old Scandinavian

The Stonehouse Inn (Ref: 160587)

The David & Charles Britain series is an exciting range of books covering The Lake District, The Peak District, The Northumbrian Uplands, The Pembrokeshire Coast National Park, and Snowdonia. There are several others planned.

Each volume – written out of deep personal knowledge of the area – provides a thorough background and guide to archaeology, natural history, the development of the landscape, and architectural styles. Each book is at least 200 pages, hardback and illustrated in colour. Buy them from your bookshop or write to us at Brunel House, Newton Abbot, Devon TQ12 4PU.

The Aire and Calder Navigation in 1715 (Picture: Leeds City Libraries)

gata in its north country meaning of "right of pasturage for cattle".

The place-name ending *ley* is very common in the region covered by Landranger Map 104. It is from an Old English word *leah* which can mean either "wood" or "clearing". Which of the two meanings is correct in any particular case can often be judged by the other elements in the name.

An example lies in *Wheatley*, the former name of *Ben Rhydding* (130470), which is the "leah where wheat was grown". Obviously *ley* must mean a "glade or clearing" in this example. Wheat doesn't grow in woods.

A similar argument applies to *Shipley* (150380), the "sheep leah", and *Calverley* (250370) the "calves leah". Evidently the name applies to a pasture in a glade in these examples.

In many cases, however, we get no such assistance because of the Anglo-Saxon habit of commonly naming places by their owners. *Ilkley* (110480) is "Illica's leah", *Otley* (200460) is "Otta's leah", *Keighley* (060410) is "Cyhha's leah", *Guiseley* (190420) is "Gislica's leah" and *Headingley* (280360) is the "leah of Hedda's people". *Batley* (240240) is "Bata's leah", *Alwoodley* (310400) is "Athelwald's leah" and *Morley* (270280) is the "leah by the moor".

The place-name element *don* often comes from the Old English word *dun* which means "hill". *Yeadon* (210410) means the "high hill", *Rawdon* (210400) means the "red hill" and *Baildon* (150390) is the "berry hill".

15

CANALS AND RIVERS

The two principal navigable rivers, the Aire and the Calder, were improved under an Act of 1699, so that they became linked together as the Aire and Calder Navigation. This enabled large vessels to reach Leeds and Wakefield. Over the years the system was improved, notably when it came under the control of William H. Bartholomew in the 1860s. Locks were enlarged and the Aire and Calder remains a commercial waterway. The system used can be clearly seen from the map, where the wavering lines of the natural river – the Aire, joining the map at 400278, the Calder at 400253 – contrast with the straight lines of the artificial cutting. The navigation alternates sections which use the natural river, for example on the Aire above the lock at 309330, with their canalised sections. Navigation ends at Leeds, but the river does provide one city-spectacular as it roars through the Arches beneath the station (298332).

The Calder leaves the map at 348200 on its way into Wakefield, but this is not the end of navigation. It was continued via the Calder and Hebble Navigation as far as Sowerby Bridge (0623). This was built under the direction of the great engineer, John Smeaton. He drew up his plans in 1757. Two years later work started and it was open in 1764 but not, alas, for long. In 1768, a devastating flood swept over the river and destroyed the locks – and, as a result, it all had to be done again. A short branch leads up to Savile Town Wharf in Dewsbury (248209) where there were stables and a blacksmith's shop for the horses that pulled the boats. The buildings now house a canal museum.

There was a limit to the possible improvements of natural waterways, so the eighteenth century solution was to build wholly artificial canals. The route of the Calder was followed westward and on through the Pennines to Manchester via the Rochdale Canal. Work began in 1794 under the direction of the engineer, William Jessop, and the Rochdale counts as one of the great achievements of the canal age, climbing up the narrow valley through the hills which must eventually be crossed. Sadly, the canal fell into dereliction but is currently being restored and the towpath provides an excellent route for walkers – with the added advantage of railway stations all along the route for a return to the starting place. Sowerby Bridge itself has a basin surrounded by fine warehouses, notable for their "boat holes", arches under which boats could be floated for loading in the dry. It is now home to a hire boat fleet. Once clear of the town, the canal threads a way through mill villages and towns, interspersed with superb Pennine scenery. There is one other canal that connects with the Calder and Hebble. Sir John Ramsden's or Huddersfield Broad Canal, was a privately financed waterway that appears briefly at 178203, heading for Huddersfield.

The first, and largest, of the trans-Pennine routes was the Leeds and Liverpool Canal – first in the sense that it was the first to be begun, in 1770. It avoided the worst of the Pennine problems by taking a very circuitous route. Liverpool lies to the south west of Leeds, but the canal can be seen leaving the map at 000483 heading north west. It was a waterway plagued by problems all through construction, mostly financial, which is why it was not completed until 1816. It is, however, a beautiful and spectacular waterway and this section contains one of its most famous features.

The route begins where the Aire and Calder stops, in the heart of Leeds and provides a surprisingly green corridor out of the city. It stays very close to the river. It is interesting to compare the alternative taken by later railway engineers. At 186387, the lines cross the railway heading west into Thackley tunnel, while the canal swings away to the north and goes all the way round the wooded hillside. At Saltaire it passes right through the great mill complex (see p.33) but soon begins to climb the valley in ever larger steps. First comes a single lock (132382). Then come two locks which are run together so that a boat going up passes straight out of the first lock and into the second (120383). The next set (107395) consists of a staircase of three inter-connected locks and the grand finale arrives at Bingley with the Bingley Five (108400). These five broad locks lift the canal 60 feet (18.3 metres) up the hillside. Apart from being a magnificent sight, they also provide an interesting exercise in logic, working out the sequence of operations to get a boat to the top. Relief comes to hard-pressed boaters after that, for the rest of the route shown on this map is lock free – it is, in fact, over 27km to the next lock. It is not altogether work-free travel as the canal is crossed by a number of swing-bridges which have to be man-handled to one side. It is, however, a most attractive route which keeps to the hillside above the Aire valley.

The other major river, the Wharfe, running south from 048600 is not navigable, but there are beautiful riverside walks, particularly above Bolton Priory, where the river is squeezed into a tumultuous cascade through the rocks of The Strid (065564). The Nidd has a popular boating centre at Knaresborough, under the shadow of the great viaduct (348570).

Reservoir facilities

b boating   f fishing
bw birdwatching

Beaverdyke 225545   f, bw
Chelker 055515   f
Dean Head, Lower & Upper 025305   bw
Embsay 545545   f, b
Eccup 300416   bw
Lindley Wood 215492   f, bw
Ogden 063308   bw
Swinsty 197533   f, bw
Ten Acre 248534   bw, f
Thruscross 150578   b, bw, f

Navigable waterways

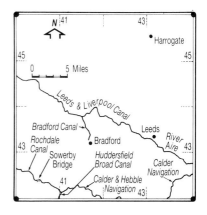

17

CASTLES, CHURCHES, HALLS

Bardsey Church of All Hallows (3643) has a tall, unbuttressed west tower with two twin bell openings. This is Anglo-Saxon but with a top which is wider and Perpendicular (1335–1530). To this original church the Normans added aisles and a fine doorway. There is the motte of a castle to the north, on Castle Hill.

There are about 150 Anglo-Saxon crosses in West Yorkshire including those at Ilkley, Otley, Collingham – the Apostles' Cross (3946), Dewsbury (2422), Leeds – St Peter being 'the most ambitious cross', Hartshead (1823), Birstall (2226) and Rastrick (1321).

Harewood Castle (3245) was originally built in the 12th century and reconstructed by Sir William Aldburg, messenger to Edward, King of Scotland, in 1367, the year when the castle was licensed for fortification by Edward III. This was the family residence in medieval times but later the Gascoigne family built and inhabited Gawthorpe, which was succeeded by Harewood House. The castle is rectangular with four-storey corner towers, two of which are now gone. The entrance was in the northwest tower which also has the portcullis chamber and the chapel. Within was the Great Hall, parts of which remain.

Knaresborough Castle (3457) was built by Serlo de Berg who received an estate of land from William I. The present castle with two baileys, however, dates from 1310–40 and some of the walls are still 12m high. The curtain walls had corner towers and the rectangular keep abutted the North curtain wall.

Leeds Castle was built shortly following the Conquest by Roger de Paganel in an area bounded by Boar Lane, Bishopgate and Millhill. Richard II (1367–1400, King 1377–1399) endured the misfortune of being imprisoned here before his mysterious and untimely death in Pontefract Castle in 1400. A Castle Folly has been built near the lake in Roundhay Park (3338).

Adel Church of St John (2740) is one of the best examples of a Norman church. It has a nave with a bell cote (of 1839) and a chancel with a lower roof line. The South doorway projects outwards to simulate a porch. There is delightful stone carving on some of the capitals.

Bradford Cathedral of St Peter was the parish church until 1919. There is some evidence that the piers of the South arcade are

Puritan Chapel founded 1649 near Branhope
(Ref: 2443. Picture: R. McConnell)

> David & Charles produce a wide ranging list of books covering every aspect of the British countryside. The full catalogue is £1 but write to us at Brunel House, Newton Abbot, Devon TQ12 4PU and we will send you a copy with our compliments.

Bolton Priory (Ref: 074542)

Norman. Much of the church was rebuilt soon after a fire in 1327 when the eight-bay arcades were constructed. The West tower, with battlements and pinnacles, and the nave are Perpendicular. Further reconstructions have been made in the 19th and 20th centuries. Inside the cathedral there is a square piece of Anglo-Saxon stone with interlace pattern.

Leathley Church of St Oswald (2347) has a tall unbuttressed Norman West tower. The bell openings are single-arched windows and the West doorway is especially narrow. Much of the remainder is reconstruction and the nave with aisles and chancel is Perpendicular.

Otley Church of All Saints has a Norman doorway and Norman windows in the chancel. The remainder is largely Perpendicular but there are 17 Saxon cross fragments. In the distant churchyard there is a small-scale tunnel model as a monument to those killed whilst constructing the Bramhope railway tunnel (2442) in 1845–9.

Spofforth Castle (3551) was a fortified house licensed in 1308 for Henry Percy and formerly part of a quadrangle of buildings. The ground floor consisted of several rooms including the kitchen. Above were the principal rooms including the Great Hall, which because of the land heights, can be entered direct from the east side.

Leeds Parish Church of St Peter was built in 1838–41 and has a large North tower, with battlements and pinnacles, and nave and chancel, both with aisles. The style is Victorian but with some Decorated (1290–1350) and Perpendicular features. There are galleries and the entrance into the North door aesthetically conflicts with the established east–west axis. The monument to Roger Holt Leigh who died in 1831 is by Sir Richard Westmacott.

The Cathedral of St Anne (R.C.) was built from 1902–4 of Gothic style. It has a North tower, nave with aisles, chancel and galleries. The reredos behind the South chancel chapel altar was designed by A. W. N. Pugin.

Wakefield Cathedral of All Saints was a Perpendicular parish church until 1888. The 80m West tower and spire have buttresses, pinnacles and crockets and were built about 1450. The arcades are complex. Two of the round North arcade piers appear to be of about 1150. The South arcade is from about 1220 and the North arcade is Decorated. However, much of the external appearance stems from the 19th century reconstructions of G. G. Scott.

Harewood House estate (3144), mentioned in relation to the castle, was bought in 1738 by Henry Lascelles, a director of the East India Company and a West Indies official. The house was built by his son, Edwin 1st Earl of Harewood, from 1759 using stone quarried on the estate. It is designed by John Carr, one of the Lascelles, with furniture by Thomas Chippendale and garden landscaping, first by Robert Adam and from 1772 by Capability Brown. The house was reconstructed in 1843–49 by Sir Charles Barry and has a South facade fronted by a terrace with a centre of seven bays and two storeys, two wings and interconnecting links. The interior is richly decorated and finely furnished despite 23 sales of works of art since World War II.

Barden Tower (0557) is a tower house, now in ruins, of Lord Clifford, reconstructed in 1659 by Lady Anne Clifford. A 17th century chapel adjoins and has a unified nave and chancel with a South tower.

East Riddlesden Hall (0842) was built in 1652 by James Murgatroyd during the Civil War with 'Vive le Roy' fearlessly inscribed on the battlements. The interior still retains the original oak panelling and plasterwork.

Cliffe Castle (0542) was rebuilt in 1874 by Henry Butterfield, a worsted manufacturer, following a gas explosion. It has a tower and gables and is now a museum displaying the geology and history of Airedale, including a domestic weaving scene.

Temple Newsam (3532) was owned by the Knights Templars in the 12–14th centuries but is now a 16th century Tudor and Jacobean red brick house with beautiful interior decor and furnishings. The grounds were landscaped by Capability Brown but suffered from recent open-cast coal mining, though now restored.

A gatehouse for Rudding Park, Follifoot (Ref: 3352. Picture: A. Kind)

RAILWAYS

Leeds is the obvious centre of the vast network shown on this map, but there is another reason for starting here – it was the site of the world's first successful steam railway. The first line was a waggonway, where horses hauled trucks over the rails, built in 1758 to link Middleton Colliery to the Aire and Calder Navigation – the first line to be approved by Act of Parliament. Then, in the Napoleonic Wars when the price of fodder was very high, the colliery manager John Blenkinsop decided to experiment with steam locomotives. He faced a real problem, however, in that the rails then in use cracked under the weight of a heavy locomotive, while a light engine was not up to the job. So he hit on the notion of adding a third toothed rail which would engage with a toothed cog on the engine – what we now know as the rack and pinion system, still used for mountain railways. A local engineer, Matthew Murray, built two engines and in 1812 the first commercial railway was at work. Among those who came to see it was a young engineer from the north-east, George Stephenson,

Crimple Viaduct on the approach to Harrogate from Leeds (Picture: A. Kind)

who began his own work with locomotives two years later.

The Blenkinsop system was soon overtaken by events and the colliery railway itself was later run with conventional rails and locomotives. The railway has one further "first" to its credit – it was the first standard gauge line to be restored and run by volunteers. So steam trains still run on this historic route, which can be seen starting at 307293. The emphasis is still quite rightly on industrial locomotives, two of which have been named after the pioneers, Blenkinsop and Murray.

Over the next few years, Leeds continued to grow and prosper, and there were early proposals to join this important manufacturing and commercial centre to the port of Hull. Eventually in 1834 a more modest line was constructed to Selby on the Ouse, where journeys were continued by river steamer. One result was that railway timetables were constantly being adjusted to keep pace with the tide tables – a practice ended by the extension of the line to Hull. There now followed two main lines for which the engineer was George Stephenson. He was not perhaps the ideal man to tackle the hilly landscape of the Pennines since he was a fervent believer in keeping to the gentlest of gradients, even at the expense of long detours, and a failure to reach important centres. Consequently the Manchester and Leeds Railway, later the Lancashire and Yorkshire (L&Y) closely followed the windings of the Calder valley. The section

Embsay Steam Railway (Picture: A. Burton)

shown here, opened in 1840, first appears at 000265, but at Sowerby Bridge it is not the passenger line heading for Halifax, but the southerly route, leaving the map at 195200 and reappearing at 334200, ending at a junction near Normanton (373215) with the second Stephenson route, the North Midland. It had been originally suggested that the two lines should both be built side by side from Normanton to Leeds, but Parliament scotched that notion and insisted that they share the last lap of the journey. The North Midland was built to join Leeds to Derby and thus provide a through route to London. The scheme, however, attracted the attention of the man who was to become known as "the Railway King", who promoted the York and North Midland, which was also to run to a junction near Normanton, and was opened in 1839.

In 1846, Leeds was joined to the other great wool town of Bradford, by which time the North Midland

Railway viaduct over the River Nidd near Harrogate (Ref: 307583. Picture: S. S. Kind)

had been absorbed into the Midland Railway, and the new line soon followed suit.

The next task facing the railway builders was to make direct connections with the centres left out by Stephenson's wandering ways. Halifax was an obvious contender, and the Leeds, Bradford and Halifax Junction Railway was begun in 1854, and was shortly joined by the Bradford, Wakefield and Leeds Railway, though the latter was in reality simply a direct Leeds–Wakefield link. The lines met at the complex junction of Wortley (2832). Both were to be taken over by the Great Northern.

The other important route was a new line to Manchester from Leeds which also gave Dewsbury a link to the latter city. It opened in 1848, together with a branch line to Batley. It was promoted by the London and North Western Railway who hoped, eventually, to gain access to Bradford as well.

The moves to the north west began with an extension of the Leeds and Bradford up the Aire valley to Keighley, from a junction at Shipley (150375). The scheme was hardly finalised before it was decided to extend the line on through Skipton to Colne in Lancashire to join the East Lancashire Railway. The line leaving the map at 000458 was opened in 1848. It was destined to be taken over by the Midland. In 1862 they promoted a branch line from Keighley to Oxenhope (032353) – the Keighley and Worth Valley Railway. The line has scarcely changed since it was opened in 1867. The stations all look much the same as they did then, and even one of the locomotives in regular use, *Bellerophon*, was built back in 1874. For this is now one of the country's most popular preserved steam railways, known also to millions who have never travelled it but have seen the film *The Railway Children*. Every effort has been made to recreate the atmosphere of the past, including the gas-lit cobbled approach to Oxenhope. The best known stop is Haworth, where the Reverend Patrick Brontë was among the first promoters of a railway down the Worth Valley and whose literary daughters have made the town world famous. The line offers passengers the full range of scenery from the little mill towns to open moorland.

The line due north out of Leeds first appeared with the completion of the Leeds and Thirsk Railway in 1848. The main engineering work on the line was Bramhope tunnel (242407 to 257438). The northern entrance is particularly fine with castellation and towers, one of which formed a picturesque if uncomfortable home for the tunnel keeper. The tunnel is reproduced in miniature in Otley churchyard (202455) as a memorial to the navvies who lost their lives in the construction. The line now ends as a disused line, between 317521 and 300600. The reason for the change centres on the lines around Harrogate. It was first reached via a branch of the York and North Midland, opened in 1847, that passed straight over the route of the Thirsk line and over the valley of Crimple Beck on an immense viaduct (320530). A diversion via a right-angled turn allowed trains from Leeds to use the viaduct into Harrogate – and still enables passengers to get a good view of it. Harrogate itself was a somewhat reluctant recipient of the railway.

Matthew Murray's engine, near Christchurch, Leeds (Picture: A. Burton)

The spa is almost surrounded by an area of open grassland, The Stray, and the local worthies did not wish it spoiled by the sight of trains. They decreed that the line must be out of sight in a deep cutting. The other line to reach Harrogate came from York. Initially it ran through Knaresborough to a junction at Starbeck with the Leeds and Thirsk (328560). The East and West Yorkshire Junction Railway was begun in 1846 and it too faced a major engineering challenge, the crossing of the deep Nidd gorge at Knaresborough. The first viaduct collapsed, blocking the river, but the replacement has given Knaresborough its famous picturesque view of the tall, castellated bridge crossing the river, echoing the style of Knaresborough's genuine Norman castle.

The link between Starbeck and Harrogate was completed in 1863.

There were a number of plans for lines up to Wharfedale, but the independent companies' plans never quite materialised and eventually an appeal was made to the two big companies in the area to sink their differences and co-operate in building a line. So the North Eastern built a line from Arthington (258445) to Otley, and the rest of the route to Ilkley (118477) was a joint venture with the Midland. The Midland followed this with a shortened route down to Shipley for a connection to Bradford. The line, running from 165457, was opened in 1876. The next obvious link was a little while in reaching completion – the extension from Ilkley to Skipton. It was not opened until 1888 but was from the first a popular tourist train: one station was at Bolton Abbey, close to the picturesque priory by the river. When passenger services were removed in 1965 this was always a likely candidate for restoration, and the Embsay Steam Railway now flourishes, based on the delightful country station (007532). The locomotives are almost all old industrial engines, at present running on two miles of track, but with the eventual aim of again reaching Bolton Abbey. Just west of Embsay is the junction with the branch line to Grassington, still used for freight and opened in 1902. Finally, completing the Wharfedale lines, the Guiseley, Yeadon and Headingley Railway was incorporated in 1891 – a grand name for a short line which merely linked Yeadon (2040) to Guiseley and from there joined the main line to Leeds. It was opened in 1893.

Inevitably such a busy manufacturing district developed a positive maze of lines, many serving particular industries. They can be seen as disused routes criss-crossing the map in the area bounded by Wakefield, Halifax, Keighley and Leeds, but space simply does not allow for them all to be listed. The areas already described are the surviving railways, and those others without which the story would not have made sense.

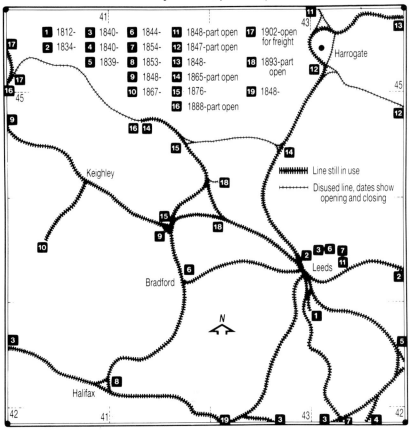

The Railway network, past and present

ANCIENT SITES

Ilkley Moor has a number of very strange ancient monuments. A large number of stones have cup-and-ring marks carved into them. One stone is preserved down by St Margaret's Church (115473) and is Bronze Age, but one of the best of the moorland stones is probably later Iron age. Known as the Swastika Stone (096470) its sinuous design suggests an Iron Age date and Celtic origins. There are Bronze Age stone circles all over the area, of which the most complete are the Twelve Apostles (127451), the Horncliffe circle (134435) and Grubstones Circle (136447). The significance of the rock carvings and the circles is not known.

In medieval times, there were two important monastic sites. Kirkstall Abbey (259362) was founded on this site by the Cistercians in 1152. If it had a different setting, other than among the industrial remains of the Aire valley, it would be undoubtedly recognised for what it is – one of the outstanding examples of Romanesque architecture. The church is almost entirely twelfth century. It is a stern building, made even more so by the blackening effect of industrial pollution. Entrance was through a massive Norman doorway, and inside are great clustered piers and rows of round-headed clerestory windows, leading to the remains of the tower. The monastic buildings are also well preserved, especially the chapter house. The gateway is now a museum (p 31).

Bolton Abbey is a village with a misleading name, for the great ruined church by the Wharfe is, in fact, Bolton Priory (074542). It was founded originally at Embsay in 1120, but moved here in 1154 and was largely completed over the next half century. It has just the romantic setting that Kirkstall lacks, and is a very popular spot. It suffered a mixed fate at the Dissolution. Work which had begun on the west tower was abandoned, but the nave of the priory church was preserved as the parish church. The west front is a particularly good example of Early English architecture.

A 'swastika'. One of the curious carvings on the rocks at Ilkley Moor (Ref: 0946)

NATURE

It is not too difficult to get away from the industrial centres of West Yorkshire to countryside which is scenically attractive and full of interest from a wildlife point of view. Indeed, the spectacular Yorkshire Dales National Park begins only some ten miles from the edge of Bradford.

Rombalds Moor (100453), which includes the famed Ilkley Moor, is almost entirely surrounded by built-up areas, and yet this open moorland of rough grassland and bracken, with some patches of heather, can still provide a notable experience for birdwatchers. All the typical birds of Pennine moorland are to be seen here, including red grouse, golden plover, dunlin, curlew and ring ouzel.

It is only to the north-west that Rombalds Moor escapes its urban ring, and here the open country leads up to the edge of the National Park. The Yorkshire Dales are best known for their stark limestone landscapes, but in this corner of the park there is some gentler, but no less attractive, countryside. Between the Barden Tower and Bolton Abbey, where the River Wharfe passes through the Strid Gorge (064564), the banks of both the main river and its tributaries are lined with woodlands supporting redstarts, pied flycatchers and woodcock. A nature trail follows the river, on which may be seen dippers and common sandpipers.

Just outside the National Park, Blubberhouses Moor drops down to the attractive Washburn Valley, where the river has been dammed to form the three large reservoirs of Fewston (188541), Swinsty and Lindley Wood, and much of the surrounding land has been afforested. The reservoirs are used as roosting areas by gulls and, over the winter, by wildfowl including wigeon, pochard, goldeneye and whooper swans. In summer, herons, curlew, redshank and snipe may be seen feeding around the water's edge, and pied flycatchers nest in the woodlands.

Penistone Hill Country Park (093367) is another expanse of

Like all buttercups, the celery-leaved buttercup has shiny yellow petals which attract pollinating insects to the many tiny stamens in the centre of the flower; each stamen develops into a seed. It has celery-like stems as well as leaves, and grows in or near slow-moving or still water.

If you live in England or Wales David & Charles have reproduced a Victorian Ordnance survey map of your area which is available for only £3.50 post and packing inclusive. You can buy it from your bookshop or write to us at Brunel House, Newton Abbot, Devon TQ12 4PU.

*The River Wharfe at Bolton Abbey, N. Yorkshire
(Ref: 0753. Picture: D. Widdicombe)*

heather moorland, lying just above the town of Haworth, and thus providing obvious inspiration to the Bronte sisters. Typical birds of the moorland include meadow pipit, skylark and whinchat. This area also supports the emperor moth, a large moth with spectacular eyespots on its wings; its green caterpillars feed on heather.

On the extreme west of the built-up area, near Mytholmroyd, the Yorkshire Wildlife Trust has a woodland nature reserve on the moorland edge, known as Broadhead Clough (000251). The wood ranges from alder and willow in marshy areas to oak and birch with occasional rowans and holly. Plants in the wetter areas include marsh violet and heath spotted orchid, whilst the woodland birds include tree pipits, redstarts and great spotted woodpeckers.

The Trust owns another site on the edge of Leeds, Adel Dam (274413), an artificial lake with birch, oak, sycamore and Scots pine woodland around it. The lake supports a good variety of birds including regular teal, mallard and heron, whilst kestrel and tawny owl are present in the woodland. Harewood Park, a few miles to the north-east, with its lake and mixed woodland, has a similar complement of birds. Both these sites probably share their bird populations with Eccup Reservoir (300418). A public footpath runs around the south side of this extensive open water area, which attracts a variety of winter wildfowl, notably goosander but also smew, wigeon and shoveler.

INDUSTRIAL ARCHAEOLOGY

The prosperity of the West Riding of Yorkshire, as the area was known for many centuries, was based on wool. The sheep grazed on the moorland and until the late eighteenth century, most of the processes of turning the fleece into cloth were carried out in the homes of the people, where the women did the spinning and the men the weaving and finishing. Towns grew up not so much as industrial centres as trading centres, epitomised by Halifax. Pieces of cloth were brought in from all the surrounding area to be sold at the market, and by 1775 it had become so prosperous that a new Piece Hall was built (095252). It is a magnificent building with galleries of offices for the merchants set around a cobbled courtyard. Today markets are still held here, but the offices are mostly shops. On site is a museum telling the story of cloth production as it was up to the time the Piece Hall was built. The Industrial Revolution had a profound effect on the textile industry. The change began with cotton but soon spread to wool. First carding and spinning were mechanised and moved from home to mill; then followed weaving and finishing. This is the story told in the adjoining Calderdale Industrial Museum. There is a collection of local machines, on which demonstrations are given. There are also re-creations of Halifax in the 1850s, with pub and pawnbroker, basement home and grocer's shop. Textiles themselves feature in Bankfield Museum, housed in a Renaissance-style building of the 1860s (092263).

There are also two rather unusual survivors from Halifax's industrial past. Cloth used to be hung out to dry on "tenter frames", hence the expression "on tenter hooks" for being in suspense. It was easy to steal – but the penalty was severe. Halifax thieves were taken to the gibbet, a device not unlike the guillotine, and had their heads chopped off. Halifax's gibbet (088254) was kept busy until the mid-seventeenth century. In the 1870s John E. Wainhouse, a dyer, built a new factory with an immensely tall chimney – over 80 metres high but it was also very grand, with an ornate stone tower surrounding the brick chimney. When the works were sold the new owner was not interested in this extravaganza, so the chimney went unused, but the tower remained – now Halifax's most prominent landmark (078240).

Leeds was, like Halifax, a commercial centre, which also became an important manufacturing centre. Armley Mills on the River Aire (276342) was once one of the world's biggest woollen mills. Built in 1806, it was originally powered by waterwheel, which still survives. Now it is an important museum showing all aspects of Leeds industrial life. There is the woollen mill, with working machinery and a clothing factory: VIPs visiting a Leeds clothier would be measured for a suit at the start of the tour and presented with the finished product at the end. There are heavy engineering exhibits and narrow gauge locomotives from the famous Hunslet works, which

Textile machinery at Bradford's Industrial Museum (Picture: A. Burton)

run on special days. The old Armley Picture Palace shows historic films. Further down the valley is Abbey House (259363), the former gatehouse of Kirkstall Abbey (p 27). It was converted to a home by the owners of the nearby iron works and is now a social history museum, with reconstructions of houses, streets, shops, a pub and workshops. Altogether there are three streets of buildings.

Thwaite Mills (328313) are very different. These were not textiles but putty manufacturers. Built in the 1820s, power came from two large waterwheels which worked crushers and rollers that pulverized rape seed to extract the oil. Local tradition has it that oil from Thwaite lubricated Stephenson's *Rocket*. The oil then formed the basis of the actual putty manufacture. The site includes the mill-owner's house.

The city has a big general museum and art gallery in the centre, but like Halifax also has its oddities. Marshall's Flax Mill (295326) was built not for wool but for linen. It was built in the style of an Egyptian temple and because the process required an even temperature, the flat roof was originally insulated by having a lawn planted on top. It was kept under control by grazing sheep! The sheep have gone, but the building survives. Almost as bizarre is a former wool warehouse in Park Square (297338). This was built in an extravagant Moorish style, complete with minarets, and is now used as offices.

Bradford, too, has a major industrial museum housed in a former woollen mill upon Moorside Road (183350). There are also transport and motive power galleries, but the main emphasis is on the machinery of the woollen and worsted industries. This is the story of a town that grew to become a city – a place where there were five steam powered mills in 1810, and 112 just thirty years later. Down in the city centre is the Wool Exchange of 1867, built like a medieval guildhall, with marble pillars and a hammerbeam roof. Another important aspect of textiles was dyeing, and a new Colour Museum in Gratten Road, allows visitors to experiment with colour as well as showing how fabrics are dyed and printed. Bradford is also home to a national museum: the National Museum of Photography, Film and Television. This exciting project offers visitors a chance to try all kinds of things for themselves, including reading the 9 o'clock news for BBC television. It covers all aspects of photographic history,

Iron bridge over the River Wharfe at Ber Rhydding (Ref: 1148)

has constantly changing displays and there are daily film shows at the IMAX cinema, with its giant 16 by 19 metre screen.

In the nineteenth century, a mayor of Bradford, Sir Titus Salt, was so disgusted with the slums of the town that he decided to build his own mill outside Bradford, on the banks of the Aire and include a model village for his employees, Saltaire (1438). The mill, which manufactured mohair, was opened in 1853 and is a magnificent example of Victorian architecture. It has now stopped work, but one section houses Gallery 1853 displaying the works of David Hockney. The town, too, has survived with all its excellent public buildings and the park supplied by Sir Titus Salt, whose statue looks out over the lawns. Here, too, is the Shipley Glen Tramway (1338) which was built in 1895, a short track providing a scenic ride. It closed in 1966 but was reopened in 1967. It still uses its old "toastrack" trams hauled by cable.

It is perhaps worth remembering that although this is a predominantly industrial region, it does have other aspects. Harrogate developed as a spa in the nineteenth century and soon became popular as a dormitory suburb for Leeds and Bradford. The story of the spa is told in the Royal Pump Room Museum (295548).

The village stocks, Follifoot (Ref: 3452. Picture: A. Kind)

TOURIST INFORMATION

Local Information Centres

Yorkshire and Humberside
Tourist Board, 312 Tadcaster Road
York YO2 2HF
(0904) 707961

Bradford
City Hall, Hall Ings, Channing Way
West Yorkshire BD1 1HY
(0274) 753678

Wakefield
Town Hall, Wood Street
West Yorkshire WF1 2HQ
(0924) 370211/370700

Halifax
Piece Hall, West Yorkshire
HX1 1RE
(0422) 68725

Knaresborough
Market Place, North Yorkshire
(0423) 866886

Ilkley
Station Road, West Yorkshire
LS29 8HA
(0943) 602319

Automobile Association
Leeds Centre, 95 The Headrow
Leeds, West Yorkshire LS1 6LU
(0532) 439090

Travel
RAC road information
Leeds (0532) 448133
Rail information
Leeds (0532) 448133
Bus information
Leeds (0532) 460011

Nature Reserves
The Royal Society for Nature Conservation (0522-752326) provides contacts for local Wildlife Trusts who can advise on the best nature reserves to visit.

Touring Companions want you to enjoy the countryside without any problems for you, other visitors, or the people who must live and work there all year round. Please remember that there is no general right to wander in the countryside, although trespass is seldom a criminal offence. Stay on the rights of way marked on the Ordnance Survey map unless there is clear indication that access is permitted, or you have asked permission. Remember that not all disused railway lines are open to the public. Always obey the Country Code.

Enjoy the countryside and respect its life and work.
Guard against all risk of fire.
Fasten all gates.
Keep your dogs under close control.
Keep to public paths across farmland.
Use gates and stiles to cross fences, hedges and walls.
Leave livestock, crops and machinery alone.
Take your litter home.
Help to keep all water clean.
Protect wildlife, plants and trees.
Take special care on country roads.
Make no unnecessary noise.

National Grid references reproduced by permission of the Ordnance Survey, Southampton.

Bingley Five Rise Locks (Ref: 1040. Picture: D. Pratt)
Temple Newsam House, Leeds (Picture: YHTB)

Authors and artists in this volume include:

A. Burton, A. & A. Heaton, S. S. Kind, D. Young, E. Danielson, S. Qureshi, J. Slocombe, A. Clift, M. Price.